COOKING
THE
BRAZILIAN
WAY

Lerner Publications Company,
A division of Lerner Publishing Group
241 First Avenue North
Minneapolis, MN 55401 U.S.A.

Website address: www.lernerbooks.com

Library of Congress Cataloging-in-Publication Data

Behnke, Alison.
    Cooking the Brazilian way / by Alison Behnke and Karin L. Duro.
        p.   cm. — (Easy menu ethnic cookbooks)
    Summary: An introduction to Brazilian cooking, featuring traditional recipes for Brazilian pork chops, black bean stew, and codfish bites. Also includes information on the history, geography, customs, and people of this South American nation.
    ISBN: 0–8225–4111–4 (lib. bdg. : alk. paper)
    1. Cookery, Brazilian—Juvenile literature. [1. Cookery, Brazilian.
2. Brazil—Social life and customs.] I. Duro, Karin L. II. Title. III. Series.
TX716.B6B39 2004
641.5981—dc22   2003015803

Manufactured in the United States of America
1 2 3 4 5 6 – JR – 09 08 07 06 05 04

COOKING

culturally authentic foods

THE

including low-fat and

BRAZILIAN

vegetarian recipes

WAY

by Alison Behnke and Karin L. Duro

ᄂ Lerner Publications Company • Minneapolis

Contents

Introduction

The South American country of Brazil is famous for its lively Carnaval celebrations and for the infectious beat of the samba, a bouncy Brazilian music and dance style that has African roots. The land itself is filled with natural beauty, from the glistening miles of sandy beaches to the green depths of the rain forests of the Amazon Basin, the region bordering the Amazon River. The people of Brazil are a varied and vibrant blend of indigenous (native), European, African, and immigrant heritages. This remarkable diversity gives Brazil another great treasure—its tantalizing cuisine, which is flavored with fiery spices and tropical ingredients. The first Brazilians used the land's native ingredients, such as black beans, squash, and the root vegetable manioc (cassava), to create hearty and nutritious dishes. European settlers brought their own tastes to the country's kitchens, introducing rice entrées and sugary desserts. African slaves later contributed coconut milk, palm oil, and hot peppers—ingredients in the popular dish *xinxim*, a rich chicken and peanut stew. In modern Brazil, cooks continue to draw on these varied influences to serve up a delicious cuisine that is uniquely Brazilian.

A true coffee cake, Brazilian bolo de café *(recipe on page 58) is flavored with the beverage for which it is named.*

The Land and Its People

The nation of Brazil sprawls across nearly half of South America, jutting eastward into the blue waters of the Atlantic Ocean. Brazil's long coast—which stretches for nearly five thousand miles—barely suggests the vastness and beauty of the country's interior. Beyond the beaches that dot the narrow coastal plains lie dramatic mountains, wide rivers, and thick rain forest.

Brazil's most mountainous area is the southeast, where the land slopes up from the coast to the peaks of the Serra do Mar range, carpeted with green. Farther inland, in the southwest, higher ground gives way to a swampy wetland region called the Pantanal. The Pantanal is home to anteaters, alligators, tropical birds, and many species of fish. A wide, flat plateau called the Brazilian Highlands stretches across central Brazil. South America's most famous feature, the Amazon River, winds through lush tropical rain forest in the northern part of the country. The mighty Amazon carries more water than any other river in the world.

Brazil's climate plays a large part in the country's life. The equator runs through northern Brazil, giving the area a tropical climate, with long, humid summers and short, mild winters. Northern Brazil is the hottest part of the country and can suffer crippling droughts. Most crops struggle in this area, although some farmers have been able to grow soybeans. Southern Brazil, especially the mountainous regions, is much cooler than the north. Heavy rains, however, make the south some of the country's best farmland. Farmers in southern and central Brazil tend thriving crops of rice, sugar, and coffee, along with fruits such as bananas, papayas, avocados, and oranges. Farmers here also raise beef cattle, chickens, and pigs.

Northern Brazil's thick rain forest leaves little room for growing crops or raising livestock. The region does benefit, however, from the abundance of fresh fish in the Amazon. Brazilians all along the eastern coast of the country also eat plenty of seafood, including lobster, shrimp, and fish.

As the fifth-largest country in the world, Brazil is home to nearly 174 million people. The earliest settlers came to the region thousands of years ago. For many centuries, these native peoples had no contact with outside visitors. Their customs and cultures included religions in which they worshiped many gods and goddesses, each representing a natural force or form. Many early Brazilians were nomads who roamed the vast, undeveloped wilderness. They hunted, fished, and gathered peanuts, cashews, bananas, pineapples, and papayas. Other groups settled in villages and began farming, planting beans, squash, and corn in the region's rich soil. Manioc, a starchy root vegetable that is also called cassava or yucca, was a valuable staple, and manioc flour formed the basis of many dishes.

In the 1500s, explorers arrived from Portugal in search of gold and silver. They introduced many European traditions to the region, including the Portuguese language and the practice of Roman Catholicism, a branch of Christianity. Colonial priests converted many of Brazil's native people to Catholicism, and the region's traditional religions almost vanished.

Portuguese colonists brought their favorite recipes with them, too, including rice—which would become a regional staple. They also brought meats such as beef and chicken, which form the basis of popular entrées such as the barbecue *churrasco*. The Portuguese also brought a taste for sweet desserts, rich with sugar and eggs. At the same time, colonial cooks began incorporating native ingredients into their recipes.

As more and more colonists arrived, they discovered that Brazil's balmy climate and fertile soil were good for growing sugarcane

Pieces of cut sugarcane

and tobacco, two crops that sold for high prices back in Portugal. Seeking workers for their plantations, colonists began to bring slaves from Africa in the 1580s. The slave trade brought great misery to Brazil, but it also brought greater diversity. African customs and music—including the samba—mingled with the native Brazilian and Portuguese cultures to form new traditions, such as the dancelike martial art *capoeira*. Slaves brought their own spiritual beliefs too. Forbidden by their Portuguese masters to practice their traditions, the slaves disguised their religion in the rituals and symbols of Catholicism. Several blends of Catholic and African beliefs resulted. One that is still commonly practiced is called *candomblé*.

Brazil's African population also added cooking methods and ingredients to the region's growing culinary mix. Slaves who worked as cooks for plantation owners had an influence on local tastes. African ingredients, including coconut milk, palm oil, and ginger, began showing up in Brazilian kitchens. Filling starchy dishes and spicy foods, such as *vatapá*—a thick puree of dried shrimp, roasted nuts, coconut milk, and spices—became Brazilian favorites.

Over the next few centuries, Brazil continued to prosper and grow. In the early 1700s, coffee plantations sprang up throughout the colony, adding another valuable farm product to the nation's exports. Then, after three hundred years of Portuguese rule, Brazil became an independent nation in 1822. In the late 1800s, Brazil's population swelled with immigrants from Italy, Germany, and Russia, who settled primarily in the country's large coastal cities. One hundred years later, immigrants from Japan, Lebanon, and Syria also made their way to Brazil. Immigrant cooks contributed their own favorite flavors to Brazil's vast array of foods. Italian pastas, German sausage, and Japanese sushi have taken their places on regional menus and in big-city restaurants. Together these varied cultures have blended to create a rich mix—one that can only be described as Brazilian.

The Food

A short list of key ingredients forms the basis of Brazilian cooking. Beans, rice, and manioc have been a big part of local cuisine for centuries. Tasty tropical fruits—such as bananas, papayas, pineapples, avocados, and oranges—also brighten Brazilian tables, alongside fresh vegetables, including collard greens, squash, yams, and eggplant.

In southern and central Brazil, the wide plains provide abundant grazing for the beef cattle favored by meat lovers. Pork and chicken dishes are also popular. In the Amazon Basin of the north, however, and all along Brazil's Atlantic coast, regional dishes are more likely to include fresh fish and seafood. Many spices and flavorings enhance all of these ingredients. Hot peppers, garlic, lemon and lime juice, coconut milk, and *dendê* oil (the oil of the dendê palm, a tree native to Africa) are staples in a Brazilian cook's pantry.

Perhaps the most typical Brazilian dish is *feijoada*, a thick stew of black beans and pork. A dish formerly prepared by slaves, feijoada has hundreds of variations, and nearly every cook has his or her favorite. Feijoada was first prepared near the southern ports of Rio de Janeiro and São Paulo, where many slaves arrived. It is often served with the traditional accompaniments *tutu*—a hearty side dish of mashed beans, onion, and garlic—and *couve*, collard greens sautéed with oil or butter. Prepared "à Mineira," or in the cooking style of the southeastern state of Minas Gerais, these three dishes date back two centuries.

Other dishes from Minas Gerais include corn, beans, pork, and cheese. In south-central Brazil, beef is more common than other meats, and meat barbecued over an open fire is a local favorite. In the northeastern state of Bahia, on the other hand, cooks along the coast make good use of fresh seafood. African influence is strong in this region too. Coconut milk livens up plain white rice, and diners use the spicy condiment vatapá, liberally.

In northern Brazil's interior, where the land is often stricken with drought, dried staples such as cornmeal, manioc, and dried meat are essential. Thick *angús*—warm cornmeal mashes that are often served with meat sauces—are popular. Northern Brazilian cuisine is also heavily influenced by indigenous cooking and makes good use of time-tested ingredients such as yams, peanuts, and fruit.

With so many influences, Brazilian cooking has its own very distinct identity. Like a complex melody that requires many musicians to work together, Brazilian food draws on each of its historical elements to create a perfect and delicious harmony.

Holidays and Festivals

Brazil is a land of celebration. Like so much of the nation's culture, holidays reflect a wide variety of traditions. Since most Brazilians are Catholic, the Christian holidays Christmas, Lent, and Easter are among the most popular.

A Christmas mural in Salvador, Brazil

For Brazilians, Christmas is a festive time for friends and family to gather, celebrate, and, of course, eat. Brazil lies in the Southern Hemisphere, so its seasons are the opposite of those north of the equator. The December holiday lands right in the middle of the Brazilian summer. Brazilians decorate their homes with flowers fresh from the garden and place clumps of soft cotton on Christmas trees for the feel of a white Christmas. Many families also set up nativity scenes, called *presépios*, showing the characters of the Christmas story.

Most families enjoy a big meal on Christmas Eve before attending the holiday Mass (Catholic church service) at midnight. Many people also go to the beach or enjoy holiday picnics on Christmas Day. Roast turkey is a traditional favorite for the Christmas meal, even during the hot summer weather! Other popular Christmas foods are roast ham, rice dishes, and *bolinhos de bacalhau* (fried codfish appetizers). Desserts with international origins, such as the Italian panettone (holiday cake) and German stollen (Christmas fruit bread) also show up on Brazilian holiday tables. On Christmas Day, children open their gifts from Papai Noel (Father Christmas), who is believed to travel all the way from Greenland. Unlike the bundled-up Santa Claus or Father Christmas in northern countries, Papai Noel dresses in a light suit to stay cool in the Brazilian heat.

In the early fall (February or March), Brazilians begin to prepare for Lent, the forty-day period before Easter. For many of the nation's Catholics, Lent is a quiet time for reflection and prayer. But before Lent begins, Brazilians have one last party, and it's a big one—the Brazilian Carnaval. Lasting for as long as a week in some regions, Carnaval is a time for dancing and feasting. Rio de Janeiro has one of the country's biggest Carnaval celebrations, and thousands of people turn out to see great parades and performances. Carnaval celebrations also include African traditions. Candomblé imagery, including dancers dressed as *Orixás* (gods and goddesses) and as candomblé priests and priestesses, plays a big part in the festivities. Musicians sing and play drums, *tamborims* (similar to tambourines),

Costumed samba school dancers line up for a Carnaval parade in Rio de Janeiro.

flutes, bells, maracas, and other instruments, providing lively samba rhythms for the hundreds of brightly costumed dancers who fill the streets. The dancers are members of samba schools, community organizations that prepare programs for Carnaval. Each school chooses a theme for its program, and the dancers act it out as they whirl around elaborately decorated floats. To feed hungry festival-goers, street vendors sell delicious snacks such as *pastéis* (sweet or savory pastries stuffed with fruit, vegetables, or meat), grilled shrimp, and sweet *bolinhos de chuva* (Brazilian doughnuts).

Compared to the music, dancing, and parties of Carnaval, Easter may seem quiet. But for devout Catholics, it is the most important holiday of the year. On Good Friday (the Friday before Easter), Catholics attend somber evening church services. And because Catholics are not supposed to eat meat on Fridays during Lent, many families have simple fish dishes for dinner. On Easter Sunday, families go to church in the morning and then celebrate with a large dinner. Kids look forward to hunting for brightly decorated eggs in their homes and yards and munching on delicious chocolate eggs.

Brazilians who practice candomblé attend festivals to honor the Orixás. These figures combine African gods and goddesses with Catholic saints. Because slaves were forbidden to observe their traditional religious rites, many Orixás' festivals came to be held on days set aside on the Catholic calendar to honor Christian saints. Other worship services celebrate many Orixás at once.

Ceremonies often take place at candomblé churches, called *terreiros*. Sometimes fireworks announce the beginning of a celebration. As worshipers gather, they make sure to honor Exú, one of the most important and mischievous Orixás. Exú is a trickster who loves to play pranks, but he is also a messenger between humans and Orixás. To be sure that he doesn't make trouble, many candomblé festivals begin with offerings to Exú of popcorn and dendê oil, which may be placed in a bowl on the floor or a table.

After the opening offering, worshipers drum, sing, and dance. Some people act as mediums, trying to communicate with the Orixás through dance and deep concentration. Each medium usually dresses as the Orixá whom he or she hopes to contact. The Orixás are very recognizable, as each has his or her own favorite things, such as colors and foods. For example, Ogun, the warrior god, favors dark blue and the symbol of a sword. The goddess of love, Oxum, prefers pastel tones and often carries flowers or mirrors in which to admire her own reflection.

The Orixás also have favorite foods. Ogun loves the hearty black bean stew feijoada, while Oxum is partial to *acarajé* (black-eyed pea fritters) and xinxim. Many of these preferred foods are prepared as offerings during

Candomblé worshipers in Brazil sweep and wash around their church. This ritual symbolizes a cleansing of the soul for a new year.

candomblé celebrations. Like Exú's popcorn, the dishes are usually set on the floor or elsewhere in the terreiro. Worshipers don't go hungry, either—they, too, enjoy these foods.

New Year's Eve is a big celebration in Brazil. Since the weather is warm and summery, the beach is a big part of the fun. In the coastal city of Rio de Janeiro, people wear white clothing, representing a fresh start for the new year, and heads to the beach. They dance, sing, and dine. Dishes often include lentils, a food that is considered lucky because of its coinlike shape. Celebrants also make offerings to the African ocean goddess Iemanjá. Brazilians of all religions light candles and send tiny boats loaded with flowers, perfume, and other gifts into the water. If an offering does not wash back up on shore, it is believed that the giver will have good fortune in the year ahead.

Other holidays in Brazil have no religious connection. Brazilians celebrate Labor Day on May 1, Independence Day on September 7, and Tiradentes Day, which honors a hero of Brazilian independence, on April 21. Many cities observe these dates with parades, fireworks, and parties. With a day off from work and school, Brazilians enjoy picnics during pleasant weather, or they may join friends and family for meals at restaurants.

However they are celebrated, all of Brazil's holidays and festivals mirror the nation's rich history and diversity. Whatever their heritage, just about all Brazilians can agree that friends and family, a soulful samba tune, and a good meal make any holiday special.

Before You Begin

Brazilian cooking makes use of some ingredients that may be new to you. Sometimes special cookware is used too, although the recipes in this book can easily be prepared with ordinary utensils and pans.

The most important thing you need to know before you start is how to be a careful cook. On the following page, you'll find a few rules that will make your cooking experience safe, fun, and easy. Next, take a look at the "dictionary" of utensils, terms, and special ingredients. You may also want to read the list of tips on preparing healthy, low-fat meals.

When you've picked out a recipe to try, read through it from beginning to end. You are then ready to shop for ingredients and to organize the cookware you will need. Once you have assembled everything, you're ready to begin cooking.

Brazilian pork chops (recipe on page 49) make a healthy, hearty main dish. Serve with collard greens (recipe on page 39) and mashed beans (recipe on page 38) for a traditional Brazilian meal.

The Careful Cook

Whenever you cook, there are certain safety rules you must always keep in mind. Even experienced cooks follow these rules when they are in the kitchen.

- Always wash your hands before handling food. Thoroughly wash all raw vegetables and fruits to remove dirt, chemicals, and insecticides.
- Wash uncooked poultry, fish, and meat under cold water.
- Use a cutting board when cutting up vegetables and fruits. Don't cut them up in your hand! And be sure to cut in a direction *away* from you and your fingers.
- Long hair or loose clothing can easily catch fire if brought near the burners of a stove. If you have long hair, tie it back before you start cooking.
- Turn all pot handles toward the back of the stove so that you will not catch your sleeves or jewelry on them. This is especially important when younger brothers and sisters are around. They could easily knock off a pot and get burned.
- Always use a pot holder to steady hot pots or to take pans out of the oven. Don't use a wet cloth on a hot pan because the steam it produces could burn you.
- Lift the lid of a steaming pot with the opening away from you so that you will not get burned.
- If you get burned, hold the burn under cold running water. Do not put grease or butter on it. Cold water helps to take the heat out, but grease or butter will only keep it in.
- If grease or cooking oil catches fire, throw baking soda or salt at the bottom of the flame to put it out. (Water will *not* put out a grease fire.) Call for help, and try to turn all the stove burners to "off."

Cooking Utensils

food processor—An electric appliance used to chop, dice, grind, or purée food

pastry brush—A small brush used for coating food or cooking equipment with melted butter or other liquids

slotted spoon—A spoon with small openings in the bowl. It is often used to remove solid food from a liquid.

strainer—A bowl-shaped mesh utensil used to drain liquid from a food, to separate fine pieces of food from larger pieces, or to sift dry ingredients such as flour and sugar

whisk—A small wire utensil used for beating foods by hand

wire rack—An open wire stand on which hot food is cooled

Cooking Terms

beat—To stir rapidly in a circular motion

boil—To heat a liquid over high heat until bubbles form and rise rapidly to the surface

brown—To cook food quickly over high heat so that the surface turns an even brown

drain—To remove liquid from a food

fold—To blend an ingredient with other ingredients by using a gentle overturning motion instead of by stirring or beating

garnish—To decorate a dish with a small piece of food such as parsley

grate—To cut into tiny pieces by rubbing food against a grater

pinch—A very small amount, usually what you can pick up between your thumb and first finger

preheat—To allow an oven to warm up to a certain temperature before putting food into it

sauté—To fry quickly over high heat in oil or fat, stirring or turning the food to prevent burning

seed—To remove seeds from a fruit or vegetable

shred—To cut or tear into thin strips by hand or with a cheese grater

simmer—To cook over low heat in liquid kept just below its boiling point. Bubbles may occasionally rise to the surface.

Special Ingredients

abóbora—Brazilian pumpkin. *Abóbora* is a member of the squash family. If abóbora is not available, use acorn or butternut squash instead.

bay leaves—The dried leaves of the bay (also called laurel) tree

carne seca—Cured and salted beef that has been dried. *Carne seca* must be soaked for at least eight hours before being used.

cilantro—An herb used fresh or dried as a flavoring and garnish

cinnamon—A spice made from the bark of a tree in the laurel family. Cinnamon is available ground or in sticks.

coconut milk—A rich liquid made by simmering shredded coconut meat with milk or water.

dendê oil—The strongly flavored oil from the dendê palm tree, native to Africa. Latin American, Caribbean, and African markets may carry dendê oil. If you can't find dendê oil, you can substitute peanut, vegetable, olive, or another cooking oil, but the taste will not be quite the same.

garlic—An herb that grows in bulbs and has a distinctive flavor that is used in many dishes. Each bulb can be broken into several sections called cloves. Most recipes use only one or two cloves. Before you chop a clove of garlic, remove its papery covering.

gingerroot—A knobby, light brown root used to flavor food. To use fresh gingerroot, slice off the amount called for, peel off the skin with a vegetable peeler, and grate the flesh. Freeze the rest of the root for future use. Fresh ginger has a very intense taste, so use it sparingly. (Do not substitute dried ground ginger in a recipe calling for fresh ginger, as the taste is very different.)

hearts of palm—The tender stems of certain palm trees. Hearts of palm are available in the canned food section of most grocery stores.

malagueta—A chili, or hot pepper, favored by many Brazilian cooks. You may be able to find fresh or preserved *malagueta* at Latin American or Asian markets. If you have trouble finding it, you can substitute fresh poblano, Anaheim, jalapeño, or other hot peppers for this chili. If you do not eat spicy food very often, try a milder pepper, such as poblano or Anaheim, before moving on to hotter chilies.

manioc—A tuber (root vegetable), similar to the potato. Also called cassava or yucca, manioc can be baked, mashed, or fried. It is also made into flours and starches that are staples of Brazilian cooking. Manioc flour, called *farinha de mandioca* in Portuguese, is a relatively coarse meal made by drying and grinding the entire tuber. Manioc starch, called *polvilho*, is a finer powder that is made by a different process. Manioc starch and manioc flour cannot be substituted for one another. Latin American, Caribbean, and Asian markets often carry both products.

olive oil—An oil made by pressing olives. It is used in cooking and for dressing salads.

rice flour—A flour made from ground rice and commonly used in desserts

salt cod—Codfish that has been salted and dried to be preserved for long periods of time. Salt cod must be soaked before using. It can usually be found in the seafood or specialty section of grocery stores or at Latin American markets.

Healthy and Low-Fat Cooking Tips

Many modern cooks are concerned about preparing healthy, low-fat meals. Fortunately, there are simple ways to reduce the fat content of most dishes. Here are a few general tips for adapting the recipes in this book. Throughout the book, you'll also find specific suggestions for individual recipes—and don't worry, they'll still taste delicious!

Many recipes call for oil to sauté ingredients. You can reduce the amount of oil you use or substitute a low-fat cooking spray for oil. Sprinkling a little salt on vegetables brings out their natural juices, so less oil is needed. Use a small, nonstick frying pan if you decide to use less oil than the recipe calls for. When recipes call for deep-frying, you may want to experiment with baking the dish instead to reduce fat. Many Brazilian dishes call for coconut milk. This flavorful ingredient has a high fat content, but you can easily cut back on fat by substituting light coconut milk.

Some Brazilian recipes call for dairy and egg products. An easy way to trim fat is to use skim milk in place of whole or 2 percent milk. In recipes that call for condensed milk, try substituting low-fat or nonfat condensed milk. When using cheese, look for reduced-fat or nonfat varieties. Eggs can be replaced with reduced-fat egg substitutes.

Brazilian cooking traditionally uses a lot of meat. Buying extra-lean meats and trimming off as much fat as possible are two simple ways to keep meals healthy. Cutting meat out of a dish altogether is another simple solution. If you want to keep a source of protein in your dish, try using a vegetarian ingredient, such as tofu or mock duck. However, since these substitutions will change a dish's flavor, you may need to experiment a little bit to decide if you like them.

There are many ways to prepare Brazilian meals that are good for you and still taste great. As you become a more experienced cook, experiment with recipes and substitutions to find the best methods.

METRIC CONVERSIONS

Cooks in the United States measure both liquid and solid ingredients using standard containers based on the 8-ounce cup and the tablespoon. These measurements are based on volume, while the metric system of measurement is based on both weight (for solids) and volume (for liquids). To convert from U.S. fluid tablespoons, ounces, quarts, and so forth to metric liters is a straightforward conversion, using the chart below. However, since solids have different weights—one cup of rice does not weigh the same as one cup of grated cheese, for example—many cooks who use the metric system have kitchen scales to weigh different ingredients. The chart below will give you a good starting point for basic conversions to the metric system.

MASS (weight)

1 ounce (oz.)	=	28.0 grams (g)
8 ounces	=	227.0 grams
1 pound (lb.) or 16 ounces	=	0.45 kilograms (kg)
2.2 pounds	=	1.0 kilogram

LIQUID VOLUME

1 teaspoon (tsp.)	=	5.0 milliliters (ml)
1 tablespoon (tbsp.)	=	15.0 milliliters
1 fluid ounce (oz.)	=	30.0 milliliters
1 cup (c.)	=	240 milliliters
1 pint (pt.)	=	480 milliliters
1 quart (qt.)	=	0.95 liters (l)
1 gallon (gal.)	=	3.80 liters

LENGTH

¼ inch (in.)	=	0.6 centimeters (cm)
½ inch	=	1.25 centimeters
1 inch	=	2.5 centimeters

TEMPERATURE

212°F	=	100°C (boiling point of water)
225°F	=	110°C
250°F	=	120°C
275°F	=	135°C
300°F	=	150°C
325°F	=	160°C
350°F	=	180°C
375°F	=	190°C
400°F	=	200°C

(To convert temperature in Fahrenheit to Celsius, subtract 32 and multiply by .56)

PAN SIZES

8-inch cake pan	=	20 x 4-centimeter cake pan
9-inch cake pan	=	23 x 3.5-centimeter cake pan
11 x 7-inch baking pan	=	28 x 18-centimeter baking pan
13 x 9-inch baking pan	=	32.5 x 23-centimeter baking pan
9 x 5-inch loaf pan	=	23 x 13-centimeter loaf pan
2-quart casserole	=	2-liter casserole

A Brazilian Table

Whether set for a formal dinner or a simple family meal, a Brazilian table is always prepared with care. An elegant bouquet of fresh flowers often brightens a table. The diners themselves carefully observe table manners. Brazilians almost always use forks and knives, even when they eat pizza or sandwiches. And, no matter how good the meal is, good company and conversation are the real focus of a Brazilian meal.

Brazilian breakfasts are simple and light, often little more than *café com leite* (coffee with milk), bread, and a piece of fresh fruit. The leisurely midday meal, called *almoço*, is traditionally the largest meal of the day. Courses may include salad, rice, beans, or potatoes, and a main entrée of meat or fish. Diners love to linger at the table, chatting and sipping coffee, long after they have finished eating. Modern workdays and busy schedules have shortened the almoço in many homes. But a Brazilian meal remains a treasured time for people to take a break and catch up with friends and family. *Jantar*, the evening meal, is eaten late and is generally a smaller, simpler meal, sometimes made up of only soup and a dessert.

Women prepare a traditional meal in Salvador, and a rose in a vase is ready for the table they will set.

A Brazilian Menu

Below are suggested menus for a substantial Brazilian lunch and a lighter dinner, along with shopping lists of the ingredients you'll need to prepare these meals. These are just a few possible combinations of dishes and flavors. As you gain more experience with Brazilian cooking, you may enjoy designing your own menus and meal plans.

LUNCH

Brazilian pork chops

White rice

Mashed beans

Collard greens

Cornstarch cookies

SHOPPING LIST:

Produce

2 medium onions
2 lb. fresh collard greens
1 bulb garlic
1 lemon
1 hot pepper (optional)

Dairy/Egg/Meat

2 sticks unsalted butter
1 egg
4 to 6 lean pork chops
(about 1 lb.)

Canned/Bottled/Boxed

olive oil
3 c. canned beans (such as
black, kidney, navy, pinto,
or great northern beans)
2 c. cornstarch

Miscellaneous

2 c. long-grain white rice
¾ c. manioc meal
sugar
salt
pepper

DINNER

Pumpkin soup

Cornmeal mash

Coffee cake

Produce

2 lb. Brazilian pumpkin, or
   acorn or butternut squash
1 onion
1 bulb garlic
1 malagueta or other hot
   pepper (optional)
fresh parsley (optional)

Dairy/Egg/Meat

1 lb. butter
grated Parmesan cheese
   (optional)
4 eggs

Canned/Bottled/Boxed

olive oil
14-oz. can diced tomatoes
32-oz. can vegetable broth

Miscellaneous

1 c. fine or stone-ground
   cornmeal
sugar
brown sugar
all-purpose flour
rice flour
coffee
instant coffee powder
cocoa powder
baking powder
salt
pepper

Staples

A Brazilian menu almost always includes a few basic staples. Farofa, a toasted manioc flour that has been popular since the time of Brazil's first settlers, is a condiment that Brazilians sprinkle on many dishes, including feijoada and xinxim. Cooks sometimes dress up manioc flour with other ingredients to create flavorful farofas.

Rice, another ever-present dish on Brazilian menus, was introduced by Portuguese colonists and quickly became an important part of most meals. It is prepared in a variety of ways, such as lightly sweetened with coconut milk or flavored with onions and tomatoes, and is often combined with favorites such as black beans. Other standards are angú (a starchy dish made from cornmeal and butter) and rich vatapá, both African in origin. These dishes form the basis of Brazilian meals, complementing any meal's entrée.

Farofa (recipe on page 32), a mainstay of the Brazilian table, can be garnished with olives and hard-boiled eggs.

Toasted Manioc Flour/*Farofa*

In many Brazilian homes and restaurants, a dish of farofa is always on the table, ready to be sprinkled on any dish. Cooks prepare a wide variety of farofas, which may be as simple as manioc flour toasted in dendê oil or may include other ingredients, such as olives, onions, nuts, or raisins.

2 tbsp. dendê oil* or butter

1 medium onion, thinly sliced

1 egg, lightly beaten

1½ c. manioc meal*

1 tsp. salt

1 tbsp. fresh parsley, chopped

6 to 8 green olives with pimentos, sliced

3 hard-boiled eggs, cubed**

1. Place oil or butter in a heavy skillet over medium-high heat.

2. Add onion slices and sauté, stirring constantly, for 5 minutes, or until onion softens.

3. Reduce heat to low and add beaten egg, still stirring constantly. Slowly stir in manioc meal and cook, stirring occasionally, for 8 minutes, or until flour is toasted to a golden brown.

4. Stir in salt and parsley.

5. Remove from heat, place in a small dish, and garnish with the olives and eggs.

*Check Latin American, Caribbean, or African markets for dendê oil and manioc meal—also called farinha de mandioca. If you can't find manioc meal, you can substitute farina, or Cream of Wheat. While these substitutions aren't completely authentic, they'll still give you a taste of Brazil. Peanut oil or vegetable oil can be used in place of dendê oil.

**Hard boil eggs by placing them in a saucepan and covering them with cold water. Place over medium heat until boiling, reduce heat, and simmer for 10 minutes. Drain water from saucepan and run cold water over eggs until they are cool. Peel and cut.

Preparation time: 10 minutes
Cooking time: 10 minutes
Serves 6 to 8

White Rice / Arroz Branco

Rice is a part of nearly every Brazilian meal. Local cooks often serve this simple dish, lightly fla-vored with onion and garlic, in place of plain white rice. Serve as an accompaniment to seafood dishes such as moqueca de peixe *(fish stew) or* xinxim *(chicken, shrimp, and peanut stew). (Recipes on pages 48 and 50).*

2 c. long-grain white rice

2 tbsp. olive oil

1 medium onion, chopped

2 cloves garlic, peeled and minced

4 c. water

1 tsp. salt

1. In a fine mesh strainer, wash rice in cold water until water draining through rice runs almost clear.

2. In a large saucepan, heat oil over medium-high heat. Add onion and garlic and sauté 2 to 3 minutes, or until garlic is just beginning to brown.

3. Add rice to saucepan* and stir to coat grains with oil. Sauté 3 to 5 minutes longer, stirring constantly.

4. Add water and salt and bring to a boil. Reduce heat to medium. Cover pan and simmer 15 to 20 minutes, or until all the water is absorbed and the rice is tender. If liquid is gone before rice is done, add more water as necessary.

5. Fluff with a fork and serve hot.

Preparation time: 15 minutes
Cooking time: 20 to 30 minutes
Serves 4

*For extra color and flavor, add one or two chopped tomatoes to the pan at the same time as the rice. Another tasty variation is to make coconut rice. Simply boil 2 c. rice with 4 c. coconut milk and a dash of salt until the liquid is gone and the rice is tender. Garnish with fresh parsley.

Cornmeal Mash/Angú

Like farofa, this starchy dish has a simple base and countless variations. Introduced to Brazilian cuisine by African slaves, angú remains a versatile Brazilian staple.

1 c. fine or stone-ground cornmeal

3 c. water

3 tbsp. butter

1 tsp. salt

1. In a small bowl, whisk together cornmeal and 1 c. of the water. Set aside.

2. Use about ½ tbsp. of butter to grease a 9-inch round pie plate. Set aside.

3. In a medium saucepan, bring remaining 2 c. water to a boil and add salt.

4. Add cornmeal mixture to the saucepan. Lower heat to medium and cook, stirring constantly, for 15 to 25 minutes, or until the mixture thickens and holds its shape. Stir in remaining 2½ tbsp. butter.

5. Pour cornmeal batter into the prepared pie plate and let sit 10 to 15 minutes, or until slightly cooled. Turn pie plate upside down onto a platter to gently remove angú. Cut in wedges and serve.*

Preparation time: 5 minutes
Cooking time: 25 to 35 minutes
(plus 10 to 15 minutes cooling time)
Serves 4

*Try serving angú with tomato sauce, meat sauce, grated cheese, or other toppings.

Shrimp and Peanut Sauce / Vatapá

Vatapá is a must-have for Brazilian diners in Bahia, a state in eastern Brazil. Rich and heavily spiced, it is often served with white rice as an accompaniment to many dishes. Look for dried shrimp, one of the crucial ingredients, at Asian or Latin American markets. Serve with farofa and white rice. (Recipes on pages 32 and 33.)

1 large loaf Italian or French bread, dried in a paper bag at room temperature for three days

½ c. dried shrimp, shelled

½ c. mixed raw (not roasted), unsalted peanuts and cashews, roughly chopped

1½-in. piece fresh gingerroot, peeled and coarsely chopped

1 onion, chopped

½ c. dendê or peanut oil

1 c. coconut milk

1 tbsp. fresh cilantro

salt to taste

preserved malagueta pepper or hot pepper sauce to taste (optional)*

1. Tear bread into chunks and soak in water in a large bowl for at least an hour. Remove and squeeze dry.

2. Combine all ingredients in a food processor or blender and process until the mixture is pastelike.

3. Transfer mixture to a medium-sized saucepan and cook over medium-low heat, stirring constantly, for 10 to 15 minutes, or until smooth and creamy. If the mixture is too thick, stir in a little bit of water.

Preparation time: 10 to 15 minutes
(plus 1 hour soaking time)
Cooking time: 10 to 15 minutes
Serves 4 to 6

*Many Brazilian dishes get their spiciness from fresh or preserved malagueta peppers. Check Latin American markets for malagueta. If you can't find it but still want to add some kick to your vatapá, you can substitute a few drops of hot pepper sauce.

Starters and Side Dishes

Brazilian cooking is full of delicious appetizers, which are enjoyed as snacks throughout the day and served as side dishes to accompany entrées. Many of these tempting extras are starch based, with mild flavors that complement stronger tasting main dishes. Spicier treats such as black-eyed pea fritters, beef dumplings, or stuffed pastries are favorites too. Variations on rice and beans are very popular and provide diners with complete, healthy protein in one delicious and low-fat dish. Simple vegetable dishes made with local produce such as collard greens, squash, or yams add a fresh flavor to any meal.

Brazilian cooks often prepare these dishes to round out meals that focus on meat or seafood entrées. However, try serving several of these side dishes in larger portions. Add a simple green salad and a loaf of crusty bread to create a wonderful and satisfying vegetarian meal.

Mild mashed beans (top) and collard greens (bottom) complement richly flavored main dishes (recipes on pages 38 and 39).

Mashed Beans / *Tutu à Mineira*

This bean dish is prepared "à Mineira," or in the style of cooking from Minas Gerais, a southeastern state of Brazil. It is usually served with collard greens and pork chops. (Recipes on pages 39 and 49).

3 c. canned beans*

2 tbsp. olive oil

1 medium onion, chopped finely

2 cloves garlic, peeled and minced

¾ c. manioc flour

salt and pepper to taste

*Many kinds of beans work well for this recipe, including black beans, kidney beans, navy beans, pinto beans, and great northern beans.

**For variety, some cooks like to sauté a chopped green pepper and chopped tomato with the onion. If you add these ingredients, sauté the mixture for an extra minute or two before adding the garlic in Step 3.

1. Drain beans over a bowl and reserve the liquid.

2. Place beans in a food processor or blender about ½ c. at a time, along with a little of their liquid. Process beans until smooth. Repeat with remaining beans.

3. In a wide, deep saucepan, heat oil over medium heat. Add onion and cook 5 minutes, or until onion is translucent (clear). Add garlic and cook 1 to 2 minutes longer.**

4. Reduce heat to low and carefully add mashed beans to pan. Slowly add manioc flour, stirring constantly. Continue cooking over low heat for 10 to 15 minutes longer, adding a bit more bean liquid if the mixture is too thick. Add salt and pepper to taste and serve hot.

Preparation time: 10 minutes
Cooking time: 20 to 25 minutes
Serves 4 to 6

Collard Greens / *Couve à Mineira*

These simple, freshly cooked greens make a delicious vegetarian side dish. They may also be served as a garnish for feijoada (recipe on page 64). If you serve collard greens with feijoada, you may choose to omit the garlic and sauté the greens alone.

1 lb. fresh collard greens*

5 tbsp. olive oil or butter

2 cloves garlic, peeled and minced

salt and pepper to taste

1. Wash greens thoroughly, removing any dirt or grit. Drain well. Use paper towels to pat dry.

2. Carefully use a sharp knife to remove hard stems from the greens. Slice greens into long strips.

3. In a heavy skillet, heat oil or butter over medium heat. Add garlic and sauté for 2 to 3 minutes, or until it is just lightly browned.

4. Add greens, salt, and pepper. Stirring constantly, cook for about 4 minutes, or until greens just begin to wilt. (They will start to look droopy.) Serve immediately.

Preparation time: 5 minutes
Cooking time: 10 minutes
Serves 4

*Look for greens that are crisp, colorful, and without spots. Refrigerate them in a plastic bag until you use them. If you can't find collard greens, you can substitute kale, a very similar leafy green.

Cheese Rolls / *Pão de Queijo*

These little rolls are a big favorite in Brazil. This recipe requires manioc starch rather than manioc flour. Look for manioc starch, also called *polvilho*, at Latin American or Asian markets. Manioc starch may also be labeled as tapioca flour.

4 c. manioc starch

1 c. vegetable oil

5 eggs, beaten*

1 tsp. salt

3 c. grated cheese, such as Parmesan, mozzarella, mild cheddar, or a mixture*

1. Combine all ingredients except cheese in a food processor or blender and process until smooth.

2. Transfer mixture to a mixing bowl and add cheese. Stir well.

3. Preheat oven to 350°F. Divide cheese dough into about 30 pieces. Rub a little bit of oil on your hands and shape the dough into balls. Place balls on a baking sheet or in the compartments of a muffin tin. Bake 15 to 20 minutes, or until rolls are very lightly browned on top. Serve warm.

Preparation time: 30 minutes
Baking time: 15 to 20 minutes
Makes about 30 rolls

*To reduce fat and cholesterol in these tasty rolls, replace the eggs with egg substitute or use 5 egg whites and only 2 or 3 egg yolks, and use reduced-fat or nonfat cheeses exclusively.

Chicken and Potato Salad / Salpicão

When making this creamy salad, most Brazilian cooks include hearts of palm, which come from the stems of certain palm trees. Hearts of palm are available canned in most grocery stores, but if you have trouble finding them, the salad is just as tasty without them. Also, to save time you may want to use a cup or two of packaged shoestring potatoes instead of frying your own.

1 lb. boneless, skinless chicken breasts*

2 tbsp. olive oil

1 tsp. salt

½ tsp. pepper

4 slices of lean cooked ham, cut into thin strips (deli-sliced ham works well)

½ c. fresh or frozen and thawed green peas

2 large carrots, coarsely grated or cut into short, thin sticks

1 green apple, cut into bite-sized pieces

1 c. canned hearts of palm, drained and chopped into ½-inch pieces

½ c. regular or reduced-fat mayonnaise

3 medium potatoes

vegetable oil for frying

1. Wash chicken under cool running water and pat dry. Cut into ½-inch cubes.

2. In a heavy saucepan or skillet, heat oil over medium-high heat. Add chicken, salt, and pepper and cook 10 to 15 minutes, or until chicken is lightly browned and cooked all the way through. Remove from heat.

3. In a large bowl, combine the chicken, ham, peas, carrots, apple, and hearts of palm. Add mayonnaise and mix well.

4. Wash and peel potatoes. Grate or cut potatoes into long, thin strips. Pour about an inch of vegetable oil into a large frying pan or stockpot and heat to 350°F, or until a drop of water flicked into the pan jumps out.

*After handling raw chicken or other poultry, always remember to thoroughly wash your hands, utensils, and preparation area with hot, soapy water. Also, when checking chicken for doneness, it's a good idea to cut it open gently to make sure the meat is white (not pink) all the way through.

5. Carefully place potatoes in oil with a slotted spoon. (If they don't all fit, you can fry them in two or three batches.) Fry 10 to 12 minutes, stirring gently. When potatoes are golden brown, remove from oil with a slotted spoon and place on paper towels to drain.**

6. Just before serving, stir most of the potatoes into the salad and sprinkle a few on top.

Preparation time: 15 minutes
Cooking time: 30 minutes
Serves 6

**Cooking with hot oil is simple and safe as long as you're careful and an adult is present. Be sure to use long-handled utensils whenever possible. Stand as far back from the stove as you can and place potatoes into oil slowly to avoid splattering.

Black-Eyed Pea Fritters/ Acarajé

Served warm and crispy, these delicious appetizers are popular all over Brazil.

16 oz. canned black-eyed peas

1 large onion, chopped

salt and pepper to taste

¼ tsp. cayenne pepper (optional)

dendê or vegetable oil for frying

malagueta pepper sauce or other
   hot sauce (optional)*

**Look for malagueta pepper sauce at
Latin American markets.*

***See page 43 for a safety tip on
cooking with hot oil.*

1. Place peas in a fine mesh strainer and rinse well with cold water.

2. Place peas, onion, salt, pepper, and cayenne in a food processor or blender and process until smooth.

3. Pour 2 to 3 inches of oil into a deep skillet or stockpot. Heat to 350°F, or until a drop of water flicked into the pan jumps out.**

4. Scoop up about 1 tbsp. of the pea mixture and use your hands to shape it into a small, oval patty. Set aside on a plate. Once you've made 4 or 5 patties, use a slotted spoon to carefully place them, one by one, into the oil. Fry for about 5 minutes, turning once to brown evenly on both sides. Carefully remove from oil and drain on paper towels. Repeat until pea mixture is gone. Serve warm with malagueta pepper sauce, if desired.

Preparation time: 15 minutes
Cooking time: 20 to 30 minutes total
Makes about 20 acarajé

Main Dishes

Traditionally, most Brazilian entrées include fish or meat. In the northern part of the country, where the great Amazon River and the many miles of coastline offer an abundance of delicious fresh fish and seafood, diners enjoy these foods with most meals. Northern cooks are famous for their moqueca de peixe and other delicious seafood stews.

In central and southern Brazil, broad plains provide plenty of grazing ground for beef cattle. Farmers also raise pigs and chickens. Meat is the preferred entrée in these regions and is usually included with the midday meal. Residents of Rio de Janeiro especially love churrasco—barbecued beef, pork, chicken, or sausage.

Brazilian diners also have a great variety of vegetarian options. Many main courses can be made with meat substitutes, with starchy ingredients such as potatoes, beans, or rice, or with vegetables alone, such as squash, tomatoes, leafy greens, or eggplant. In addition, the simple but rich flavors of garlic, coconut, lemon, and hot peppers combine to make dishes with or without meat equally tasty.

Fish stew (recipe on page 48) combines the strong flavors of cilantro, lemon juice, and coconut milk to create a savory dish ideal for adventurous eaters.

Fish Stew/Moqueca de Peixe

White fish varieties, such as snapper, cod, sole, haddock, or flounder, work well for this stew. This dish, which originates in the northeastern coastal state of Bahia, is very popular throughout Brazil.

2 lb. skinless white fish fillets

1 clove garlic, peeled and minced

1 fresh hot pepper, minced, or 1
tsp. cayenne pepper (optional)*

4 tbsp. fresh cilantro, chopped

½ tsp. salt

½ tsp. black pepper

juice of 1 large lemon

1 14.5-oz. can diced tomatoes,
drained

1 medium onion, chopped

2 tbsp. dendê or olive oil

½ c. coconut milk

1. Rinse fish under cool running water and pat dry. Cut into roughly 2-inch-square pieces and place in a large mixing bowl or baking dish.

2. In a food processor or blender, combine garlic, hot pepper (if using), cilantro, salt, black pepper, lemon juice, and half of the tomatoes and onion. Process until smooth.

3. Pour the tomato mixture over the fish. Cover with plastic wrap and refrigerate for 1 hour.

4. Heat dendê or olive oil in a heavy saucepan over medium heat. Add fish, processed tomato mixture, remaining tomato and onion, and half the coconut milk.

5. Bring to a boil. Reduce heat and add remaining coconut milk. Cover and simmer 10 to 15 minutes, or until fish is cooked through. Serve hot with rice.

* Be careful when working with hot peppers or chilies. The oil on the skin of the peppers can burn you, so wear rubber gloves while cutting the pepper, and be sure to remove all the seeds. Wash your hands well when you are done.

Preparation time: 20 minutes
(plus 1 hour marinating time)
Cooking time: 25 to 30 minutes
Serves 4 to 6

Brazilian Pork Chops/ *Costeletas de Porco*

Serve hot with white rice, mashed beans, and collard greens. (Recipes on pages 33, 38, and 39.)

4 to 6 lean pork chops (about 1 lb.)

2 tbsp. olive oil

juice of 1 lemon

1 to 2 cloves garlic, peeled and minced

1 tsp. salt

1 tsp. black pepper

1 minced hot pepper (optional)*

1. Wash pork chops under cool running water and pat dry with a paper towel. Trim off any visible fat.

2. In a wide baking dish or bowl, combine all ingredients except pork chops and mix well. Add pork chops, stir well to coat, and cover dish with plastic wrap. Place in the refrigerator for at least 1 hour.

3. In a large skillet over medium-high heat, cook 3 pork chops for 5 to 7 minutes on each side. If you have 2 skillets and someone to help you, you can cook all the pork chops at once. Otherwise, carefully place the first batch on an ovenproof plate in a warm oven (about 200°F) while you cook the second batch.

Preparation time: 10 minutes
(plus 1 hour marinating time)
Cooking time: 15 to 30 minutes
Serves 4 to 6

*To give this dish extra spice, some Brazilian cooks add a finely minced hot pepper. Jalapeño, malagueta, and serrano peppers make good choices. If you are not used to eating spicy foods, begin with a small amount of chili pepper and adjust to your tastes.

Chicken, Shrimp, and Peanut Stew / Xinxim

The dendê oil, roasted nuts, and coconut milk in xinxim are flavors that were originally brought to Brazil from Africa. This rich stew is often prepared for candomblé ceremonies.

juice of 1 large lemon

2 cloves garlic, peeled and crushed

2 tsp. salt

1 tsp. pepper

4 to 6 boneless, skinless chicken breasts

2 tbsp. dendê or peanut oil

1 medium onion, chopped

1 c. chicken stock or water

½ c. roasted peanuts, very finely chopped

⅓ c. coconut milk

1 fresh hot pepper or 2 preserved hot peppers, minced (optional)

1 lb. fresh shrimp, peeled and deveined,* or 1 lb. frozen shrimp, thawed

1. In a large bowl or baking dish, combine lemon juice, garlic, salt, and pepper to make marinade.

2. Wash chicken under cool running water. Pat dry and cut into 1-inch chunks. Place chicken in marinade, cover dish with plastic wrap, and refrigerate for 30 minutes.

3. In a heavy saucepan or skillet, heat oil over medium-high heat. Add onion and chicken pieces and cook 10 minutes, or until chicken is lightly browned.

4. Add chicken stock or water, peanuts, coconut milk, and hot pepper (if using). Reduce heat to medium. Simmer, stirring occasionally, for 15 to 20 minutes, or until chicken is fully cooked and sauce has thickened. Add shrimp and cook 8 to 10 minutes more, or until shrimp are pink. If you have dendê oil, drizzle lightly over all before serving.

*You may be able to have fresh shrimp peeled and deveined at the grocery store. Otherwise, hold the shrimp with the underside facing you. Use your fingers to peel off the shell from the head toward the tail. Carefully use a sharp knife to make a shallow cut down the middle of the back. Hold the shrimp under cold running water to rinse out the dark vein.

Preparation time: 10 minutes
(plus 30 minutes marinating time)
Cooking time: 35 to 40 minutes
Serves 4 to 6

Pumpkin Soup/Quibebe

Served with crusty Italian bread, this hearty soup makes a delicious vegetarian meal. Or try serving quibebe with angú (recipe on page 34).

3 tbsp. olive oil or butter

1 onion, chopped

1 garlic clove, peeled and minced

8 oz. (1 c.) canned diced tomatoes, drained

1 fresh hot pepper, seeded and minced (optional)

2 lb. Brazilian pumpkin or squash, cut into chunks*

4 c. water or vegetable broth

¼ tsp. sugar

salt to taste

black pepper to taste

Parmesan cheese, grated (optional)

fresh parsley, chopped (optional)

1. In a medium stockpot, heat oil or butter over medium heat. Add onion, garlic, tomato, and hot pepper (if using). Cook 15 minutes, or until mixture begins to thicken.

2. Add pumpkin and water or broth and bring to a boil. Reduce heat. Add sugar, salt, and pepper and cover. Simmer 20 to 25 minutes, or until pumpkin becomes very soft and begins to break apart. Use a whisk or a potato masher to break up any remaining large chunks.

3. Serve hot, garnished with cheese and parsley if desired.

Preparation time: 30 minutes
Cooking time: 35 to 40 minutes
Serves 4 to 6

*Brazilian pumpkin, or abóbora, is more like squash than North American pumpkin. In place of genuine abóbora, acorn or butternut squash will work fine for this recipe. To use the squash, cut it in half and remove the seeds with a spoon. Carefully use a vegetable peeler or a sharp knife to remove the skin, and cut flesh into 1-in.-square chunks. Squash have thick skin and tough flesh, and they can be difficult to peel and cut. You may want to ask an adult to help you with these steps.

Desserts and Drinks

Ever since the arrival of the Portuguese, Brazilians have loved sweets. The colonists' fondness for eggs and milk, along with the local crop of sugarcane, made for delicious rich desserts. African influence made coconut another favorite ingredient, and regional delicacies such as avocado also found their way into local dessert recipes. Corn, long a mainstay of Brazilian cooking, plays a role in desserts such as cornstarch cookies and creamy corn cake. Children enjoy a variety of candies. Favorites include *olho de sogra* (coconut-stuffed prunes) and *brigadeiro*, a rich chocolate fudge treat.

Sweet drinks, such as lemonade—which, in Brazil, is actually made with limes—and other cool, refreshing fruit beverages are popular on hot summer days. Brazilians enjoy thick fruit shakes and drinks when attending Carnaval festivities.

Coconuts grow well in Brazil and show up in many traditional desserts, such as these coconut candies (recipe on page 54).

Coconut Candies / *Olhos de Sogra*

In Portuguese, olhos means "eyes," and with their smooth, white coconut filling and whole cloves for "pupils," these sweet treats do look a bit like eyeballs!

8 oz. reduced-fat condensed milk

1¼ c. sugar

3 egg yolks*

2 c. grated coconut

1 c. large pitted prunes

25 to 30 whole cloves**

*To separate an egg, have two bowls ready. Crack the egg cleanly on the edge of one bowl (nonplastic works best). Holding the two halves of the eggshell over the bowl, gently pour the egg yolk back and forth between the two halves, letting the egg white drip into the bowl and being careful not to break the yolk. When most of the egg white has been separated, place the yolk in the other bowl.

**Whole cloves are available in the spice section of the grovery store. Be sure to remove the cloves before eating!

1. In a medium saucepan, combine condensed milk and 1 c. of sugar. Cook over medium heat for 5 minutes, or until sugar has dissolved.

2. Add egg yolks and coconut to pan. Stir well and cook 10 to 15 minutes longer, stirring often, until mixture begins to thicken into a candy syrup. The syrup has the right texture when patches of the bottom of the saucepan show as you are stirring. Remove pan from heat and allow syrup to cool for 10 or 15 minutes.

3. Cut each prune into four equal pieces. Form the cooled coconut candy into egg-shaped pieces about 1 inch long and press each piece firmly onto a prune segment. Place a whole clove in the center of the visible white coconut stuffing.

4. Place remaining ¼ c. sugar in a small bowl. Roll each "eye" in sugar and serve in small paper cups.

Preparation time: 1 hour
Cooking time: 15 to 20 minutes
Makes 25 to 30 candies

Lemonade/ *Limonada*

This beverage is just one of many fresh fruit drinks enjoyed throughout Brazil.

2 small limes*

6 c. water

1 c. sugar

1. Cut each lime in half, and cut each half into four pieces.

2. In a blender, combine 3 c. of water with the unpeeled lime segments.

3. Process mixture for 2 to 3 seconds. Be careful not to overprocess, as this will give the lemonade a bitter flavor.

4. Pour the liquid into a pitcher through a sieve or strainer to remove lime peel and pulp. Add the remaining water and sugar to taste and stir well. Serve fresh, in tall glasses filled with ice.

Preparation time: 5 minutes
Serves 4

*In Brazil lemonade is almost always made with thin-skinned limes rather than lemons, whose thicker skins add bitterness to the flavor of the drink.

Avocado Cream/*Creme de Abacate*

This unusual method for preparing avocados—one of Brazil's most popular fruits for desserts—makes a cool, refreshing treat.

2 medium avocados*

¼ c. sugar

1 to 2 tbsp. fresh lime juice

2 to 4 tbsp. cold milk

1. Peel and pit avocados.

2. Place avocado, sugar, and lime juice in a food processor or blender and process until smooth. Add just enough milk to give mixture a creamy, puddinglike consistency.

3. Spoon mixture into six dessert dishes or sundae glasses. Cover and chill for at least 1 hour and serve cold.

Preparation time: 15 minutes
(plus 1 hour refrigeration)
Serves 6

*Look for avocados that are slightly soft but not mushy. If avocados are too hard to use, let them sit on a shelf or countertop for a few days until they soften. To peel and pit an avocado, carefully use a sharp knife to cut the avocado in half lengthwise, cutting around the pit. Gently twist the two halves apart and use your fingers or a spoon to remove and discard the pit. Use a spoon to scoop the avocado out of the peel.

Coffee Cake/*Bolo de Café*

As the largest coffee producer in the world, it's no surprise that Brazil also creates sweet desserts flavored with strong local coffee.

2 sticks of butter, softened

2 c. brown sugar

4 eggs, separated

2 c. all-purpose flour

1 c. rice flour*

1 c. strong coffee, or ½ c. instant coffee powder mixed with 1 c. water

1 tsp. baking powder

1 tsp. instant coffee powder

1 tsp. cocoa powder

1. Preheat oven to 350°F. Lightly grease a 9×13-inch baking pan.

2. In a large mixing bowl, combine butter and sugar and blend thoroughly.

3. Add egg yolks and beat well.

4. Add all-purpose flour, rice flour, coffee, and baking powder. Mix well.

5. In a small mixing bowl, beat egg whites until stiff. Fold into cake batter.

6. Pour batter into baking pan and bake 40 minutes, or until a toothpick inserted into the center of the cake comes out clean. Sprinkle with coffee and cocoa powders and cut into squares to serve.

Preparation time: 15 minutes
Baking time: 40 minutes
Serves 12

*Look for rice flour at Asian or Latin American markets. If you have trouble finding rice flour, you can substitute an equal amount of cornstarch for this ingredient.

Cornstarch Cookies/Biscoitos de Maizena

Cornstarch gives these simple cookies a unique flavor, and they are longtime favorites with children and adults throughout Brazil.

2 c. cornstarch

1 c. sugar

¼ tsp. salt

1 egg, beaten

1½ sticks unsalted butter, softened

1. Preheat oven to 375°F.

2. In a large mixing bowl, combine cornstarch, sugar, and salt.

3. Stir in egg and blend in softened butter.* You may find it easiest to use your hands to mix the dough at this point. Set dough aside for 15 minutes to make it easier to work with, and lightly grease a cookie sheet.

4. Form dough into very small balls, about ¾ inch in diameter. Place on cookie sheet and press down lightly with the tines of a fork.

5. Bake 12 to 18 minutes, or until lightly browned. Allow to cool slightly on the cookie sheet before removing to a wire rack to cool completely.

Preparation time: 15 to 20 minutes (plus 15 minutes sitting time)
Baking time: 12 to 18 minutes
Makes about 3 dozen cookies

*For an extra taste treat, stir in 2 oz. grated coconut when you add the butter.

Holiday and Festival Food

Brazil's diverse calendar of holidays and festivals gives the country's cooks many opportunities to prepare special dishes for special occasions. Like the occasions themselves, these dishes reflect a variety of influences and traditions. Carnaval revelers enjoy pastéis, the popular Spanish and Portuguese turnovers brought to Brazil by colonial settlers. These delicious pastries are often stuffed with chicken, beef, or other meats. Creative cooks use ingredients ranging from spicy shrimp to cinnamon-flavored pumpkin. Feijoada remains another beloved holiday favorite.

While many of the recipes in this section are associated with particular celebrations, Brazilians also enjoy them throughout the year. Prepare these dishes anytime to turn an ordinary meal with friends or family into a festive event and to celebrate the Brazilian way.

Turnovers, or pastéis (recipe on page 62), can be filled with ground meats, seafood, or vegetables.

Turnovers / Pastéis

Street vendors in Rio de Janeiro and other Brazilian cities serve hot, savory pastéis during Carnaval and other celebrations. This recipe is for chicken pastéis, which are among the most common in Brazil. However, beef and shrimp are also used, and delicious vegetarian pastéis are made with potatoes or even with sweet fillings such as fruit.

Filling:

1 tbsp. olive oil

1 small onion, chopped

1 clove garlic, peeled and minced

3 boneless, skinless chicken breasts—rinsed and patted dry

1 bay leaf

3 tbsp. tomato paste

salt and black pepper to taste

3 tbsp. all-purpose flour

8 pitted green olives, chopped

pinch cayenne pepper

1. To prepare the filling, heat oil in a large saucepan over medium heat. Add onion and garlic and cook for 2 to 3 minutes.

2. Add chicken breasts, bay leaf, tomato paste, salt, black pepper, and just enough water to cover all. Stir to combine and bring to a boil. Reduce heat, cover, and simmer 20 minutes, or until chicken is white all the way through. Remove chicken. Carefully pour remaining broth through a strainer into another pan, and reserve.

3. Using a fork and knife or your fingers, shred chicken finely. In a large mixing bowl, combine chicken, flour, olives, cayenne, and 3 to 4 tbsp. of the reserved broth. The filling should be moist, but not runny.

Pastry:

4 c. all-purpose flour

1 c. vegetable shortening, softened

1 tbsp. butter, softened

1 tsp. salt

2 eggs

1½ c. water

Glaze:

1 egg

pinch salt

4. To make pastry, place flour in a large mixing bowl. Make a hole in the middle of flour. In a second bowl, combine shortening, butter, salt, eggs, and 1 c. water. Pour this mixture into the hole in flour.

5. Use your hands to combine the ingredients, squeezing them into a paste. If dough is too stiff or hard, add a little more water. When dough has a smooth, slightly sticky texture, set aside at room temperature for 30 minutes.

6. Preheat oven to 350°F. Form dough into balls about 1½ inches in diameter. On a lightly floured countertop or other surface, roll the dough out into thin rounds 3 or 4 inches in diameter. Place about 1 tbsp. of filling into the center of each piece of dough. Fold dough over and press edges together firmly. Wet your fingers with some water to tightly seal pastry edges. Place on a greased cookie sheet about 1 inch apart.

8. To make glaze, beat egg yolk with salt in a small bowl. Use a pastry brush to lightly glaze pastéis. Bake 30 minutes, or until golden brown. Serve warm.

Preparation time: 45 to 50 minutes
(plus 30 minutes standing time)
Cooking time: 60 minutes
Makes about 45 pastéis

Black Bean Stew/*Feijoada*

This dish, served in honor of the Orixá Ogun during candomblé festivals, is also considered the national dish of Brazil. Common side dishes include white rice and collard greens (recipes on pages 33 and 39).

1 to 2 lb. assorted meats, such as mild smoked pork sausage, pork tenderloin, bacon, or carne seca (dried and salted beef)

2 tbsp. vegetable oil

1 small onion, chopped

1 to 2 cloves garlic, peeled and minced

½ tsp. salt

2 16-oz. cans black beans

5 c. water

2 bay leaves

2 oranges, cut into wedges

1. If using carne seca or salted meats, place in a large dish, cover with cold water, and soak overnight.

2. Drain and rinse salted meats. Place all meats in a large kettle or stockpot with enough water to cover. Place over medium heat, cover, and simmer, stirring occasionally, 1 to 1½ hours or until meat is tender. Add water as needed to keep meat covered.

3. In a second large kettle or stockpot, heat oil over medium heat. Add onion, garlic, and salt. Sauté 2 to 3 minutes, or until garlic begins to turn golden brown.

4. Add beans and mash slightly with a fork. Add 6 c. water and bring to a boil.

5. Add bay leaves and cooked meat. Simmer 20 to 30 minutes more. Serve feijoada hot. Garnish with orange wedges.

Preparation time: 20 minutes
(plus overnight soaking time for salted meat)
Cooking time: 1½ to 2 hours
Serves 6

Codfish Bites/*Bolinhos de Bacalhau*

Like Christmas itself, these delicious holiday appetizers came to Brazil with the Portuguese, and these appetizers remain a local favorite.

¾ lb. boneless, skinned salt cod fillets*

2 small new potatoes, washed and peeled

1 small onion, minced

1 tbsp. fresh parsley, minced

½ tsp. salt

½ tsp. pepper

2 eggs, separated

1 to 2 tbsp. all-purpose flour

vegetable oil for deep-frying

malagueta pepper sauce (optional)

*Look for salt cod in the seafood department of your local grocery store or at Latin American markets. If you cannot find boneless, skinless fillets, you can remove the bones and skins yourself after soaking. Use a sharp knife and a fork to peel the skin away from the flesh and use your fingers to remove the bones.

1. Place salt cod in a dish with enough water to cover. Cover dish with plastic wrap and refrigerate 8 hours, or overnight. If you have time, change water once or twice during soaking.

2. When fish is nearly done soaking, cut the potatoes into halves and place in a stockpot with enough water to cover by 1 inch. Bring to a boil and cook 20 minutes, or until tender. Remove from heat and let cool.

3. Meanwhile, drain cod, rinse well, and place in a medium saucepan with enough water to cover. Bring to a boil, reduce heat, and simmer for 15 minutes, or until fish is tender. Remove from heat. When fish is cool, carefully remove the bones and skin.* Chop fish into roughly ½-inch pieces.

4. Mash potatoes with a fork or potato masher and place in a large mixing bowl. Add cod, onion, parsley, salt, and pepper. Beat egg yolks in a small bowl and add to codfish mixture. Stir to combine. If mixture is runny, add 1 to 2 tbsp. flour and mix well.

5. In a small bowl, beat egg whites for about 5 or 6 minutes, or until stiff. Fold whites into codfish mixture. Cover mixture and refrigerate for 30 minutes.

6. Form codfish mixture into small balls, about 1 to 1½ inches in diameter. Pour about 2 inches of oil into a deep kettle or frying pan. Heat to 350°F, or until a drop of water flicked into the pan jumps out.

7. Use a slotted spoon to place 4 or 5 balls into the oil. Fry for 3 to 5 minutes, or until golden brown all over. Remove from oil and drain on paper towels. Serve hot, with malagueta pepper sauce for dipping, if desired.

Preparation time: 1 hour
(plus overnight soaking time and 30 minutes refrigeration)
Cooking time: 1 hour
Makes 20 to 24 bolinhos

Cinnamon Doughnuts/*Bolinhos de Chuva*

These cinnamon-sprinkled delights are a popular snack for Carnaval-goers with a sweet tooth.

2 large eggs

½ c. plus 3 tbsp. sugar

pinch salt

1 c. all-purpose flour

½ c. cornstarch

2 tsp. baking powder

½ c. milk, warmed slightly to room temperature

vegetable shortening for deep frying

3 tbsp. cinnamon

1. In a large mixing bowl, combine eggs, ½ c. sugar, and salt. Mix well. While stirring, slowly add flour, cornstarch, baking powder, and milk.

2. Pour 2 to 3 inches of oil into a deep skillet or stockpot. Heat to 350°F, or until a drop of water flicked into the pan jumps out.

3. Carefully drop several spoonfuls of batter into the oil. Each piece of batter will make a bite-sized doughnut. Fry 3 to 4 minutes, or until evenly browned on all sides. Use a slotted spoon to remove doughnuts from oil and drain on paper towels.

4. Combine cinnamon and remaining 3 tbsp. sugar in a small bowl. When cool enough to handle, roll each doughnut in cinnamon-sugar mixture to coat and serve warm.

Preparation time: 20 minutes
Cooking time: 20 to 25 minutes
Makes about 2 dozen doughnuts

Index

About the Authors

Alison Behnke enjoys traveling and experiencing new cultures and cuisines. She has written and edited many other books, including *Cooking the Cuban Way, Vegetarian Cooking around the World, Italy in Pictures, Japan in Pictures,* and *Afghanistan in Pictures.*

Karin L. Duro was born in Belo Horizonte, Brazil. Her mother taught her how to cook, and she especially loves preparing delicious Brazilian desserts. She and her husband left Brazil in 1999, when his job brought them to the United States. Eager to prepare Brazilian food in their new home, the two started looking for their favorite ingredients in American grocery stores. They went on to create a website called *Cook Brazil,* <http://www.cookbrazil.com>, where they share Brazilian culture and recipes with people from all over the world.

Photo Acknowledgments

The photographs in this book are reproduced with the permission of: © Staffan Widstrand/CORBIS, pp. 2–3; © Joel Creed; Ecoscene/CORBIS, p. 10; © Arvind Garg/CORBIS, p. 13; © Stephanie Maze/CORBIS, pp. 15, 17; © Jeremy Horner/CORBIS, p. 26; © Walter and Louiseann Pietrowicz/September 8th Stock, pp. 4 (both), 5 (both), 6, 18, 30, 36, 41, 45, 46, 52, 56, 60, 65, 68. The illustrations on pages 7, 19, 27, 29, 31, 32, 33, 34, 35, 37, 38, 39, 40, 42, 43, 44, 47, 48, 49, 50, 51, 53, 54, 55, 57, 58, 59, 61 and 66 are by Tim Seeley. The map on page 8 is by Bill Hauser.

Cover photos (front, back, and spine): © Walter and Louiseann Pietrowicz/September 8th Stock.